I0756279

FINISHING LINE PRESS
www.finishinglinepress.com

1803

The Wintering

poems by

Mark B. Hamilton

Finishing Line Press
Georgetown, Kentucky

POETRY BY MARK B. HAMILTON

1803: The Wintering

Lake, River, Mountain

Upstream

OYO: The Beautiful River

100 Miles of Heat

Confronting the Basilisk

Earth Songs

1803

The Wintering

ISBN 979-8-89990-422-6 First Edition

ACKNOWLEDGMENTS

With thanks to the editors:

About Place Journal: "Ancient Mounds"
Copperfield Review Quarterly: "Captain Clark Is Very Sick"
The Listening Eye: "Two Days Without"
The Lyric Magazine: "Shelter," "A Gathering," and "Camp & Mess"
A Museum of Americana: A Literary Review: "The Feast"
Plainsongs: "Work Days"
Poetry Society of Virginia Newsletter: "Stores & Supply"
The Road Not Taken: "Sugar Makers"
Slant: "The Market Place, 1804"
Sparks of Calliope: "Unwell" and "Still Very Unwell"
Weber—The Contemporary West: "Sick in Bright Light" and "Potatoes, Brandy and Porter"
We Proceeded On: "An Oral History of the Mammoth in North America."

And to the production team at Finishing Line Press, Christen Kincaid, editor, and Leah Huete de Maines, publisher.

Publisher: Leah Huete de Maines
Editor: Christen Kincaid
Cover Art: Mary Hamilton Moczygemba
Author Photo: Mark B. Hamilton
Cover Design: Elizabeth Maines McCleavy

Order online: www.finishinglinepress.com
also available on amazon.com

Author inquiries and mail orders:
Finishing Line Press
PO Box 1626
Georgetown, Kentucky 40324
USA

Contents

Preface xi

A Tribute to the Romantics

Ode to Absence 1
Upon Reading Scott's *The Common Wind* 3
Ode to Causes 5
An Oral History of the Mammoth in North America 7

From the Winter Journals of Captain William Clark

Shelter 11
Under a Hazy Sun 12
Fresh Venison 14
December 25th 15
A Gathering 16
The Feast 17
Work Days 19
The Paddlers and the Swan 21
So Ends the Year 23
The Market Place, 1804 24
Establishing Order 25
Cold Work 27
Ancient Mounds 29
Unwell 31
Winter was Deep 32
Plans for Spring 34
Sick in Bright Light 35
Potatoes, Brandy and Porter 36
Visions North 38
Still Very Unwell 39

People's History at River Dubois by an Anon Narrator

Captain Clark is Very Sick 43
Two Days Without 45
Camp & Mess 48
Stores & Supply 49
Hunters 50
Sawyers 51
Blacksmiths 52

Sugar Makers 53
Voyageurs 54
Captain Lewis Returns 55
Reined-In 56
von Steuben's Drill 57
In Step with Burdens 59
Captain Lewis Departs 60
Morning Muster 61
Discipline Falls Abject 63
To Quell the Unrest 65
Abuse by Some 66

Endnotes 67

Bibliography 68

About the Author 71

—dedicated to Mary Brewer Hamilton Moczygemba,
and to the Daughters of the American Revolution

PREFACE

As author, my premise for *1803: The Wintering* is that literature, and poetry in particular, can function as a heuristic method for improving understandings of historical documents, as cultural texts with underlying meanings based upon human complexities.

Poetry, as a genre, creates a wonderful opportunity for perceiving the world through the sensibilities—as a threshold, it enthuses information with the immediacy of experience, evoking through language the reader's personal life and its depth of memory. Poems, adapted from historical events, persons, and day-to-day activities, encourage empathies that enliven explications and descriptions with contemporary perspectives. In this way, questions about the past can be answered, causes and effects can be explored. And from these intimate connections, we gain insights into commonalities experienced through time.

It is my hope to communicate the empirical data truthfully, while allowing this depth of human interaction to become evident. Poetry carries both the literal and the figurative simultaneously: the intellect with the intuition, the empirical with the emotions, and the experiential with the imagination. All combine to interact as they clarify oftentimes disparate relationships between facts and feelings, social issues and personal desires, cultural values and the wider meanings from specific events.

In history-based poetry, the objective is to capture the past in a series of immediate moments. When that door opens, we step through the past into the present. At this juncture, the historical narrative becomes both reality and consequence, and in very basic and human ways, the poetic process explores this as our cultural identity.

Through heuristic creativity, I have come to realize that working in traditional verse from historical documents is somewhat analogous to the search for ancient remnants during an archaeological dig. As time is unearthed, specifics are exposed. With each new accumulation of data, juxtapositions incur further patterns. Relationships become evident while catalogues are kept and inferences discerned. As the search finds expression, it grows into meaning from the demands of acquiring necessary constructs of language. The discoveries evoke responses, and empathies direct interpretations and conclusions. From these efforts, the poetic integrity arises, guided by research, field studies, and the expertise of scholars and other textual archeologists.

This book of verse is well-founded in the history of pre-industrial America, especially focused upon the Lewis and Clark era, and has benefited from various areas of additional study, including: First Nations cosmologies, the environment, 19th Century Literature, wood craft, boat skills, the military, and specific supporting research in: the Revolutionary War, 18th Century medicine, Peale's Museum, the paleontology of the mammoth, Enlightenment Science, the death of Sergeant Charles Floyd, the Chouteau Family of early St. Louis, the Voyageurs of the fur trade, and the American Naturalists.

For critical assessments of the creative process and the accuracy in adapting historical documents, several mentoring scholars have been a true and positive influence. I feel especially fortunate in thanking: Professors Harry Fritz, William Bevis, Richmond Clow, Patricia Goedicke, and Hank Harrington, University of Montana; Professors Glover Davis, Carolyn Forche, Lowell Tozer, and Mary Redding, San Diego State University; The librarians and archivists at the American Antiquarian Society and the State Historical Society of Missouri; The editors of peer-reviewed journals who offered public forums for these poems; And the contest judges in awarding this book First Honorable Mention for the 2024 Donna Wolf-Palacio Poetry Prize.

My personal response to *The Journals of the Lewis & Clark Expedition,* as edited by Gary E. Moulton, was augmented by a 3-year, 8,000-mile trek along the entire Lewis and Clark route, beginning at Pittsburgh, Pennsylvania, traveling on their approximate time-table, and as they did by paddle and pack mule. This has allowed me a certain acuity in reading Captain William Clark's written entries while at Camp Dubois.

1803: The Wintering is comprised of three sections: Section one is a tribute to the influence of the British Romantics: especially Keats and Wordsworth for recognizing Nature as the supra-context within which we all must function and live. Section two adapts Captain William Clark's winter journal entries into traditional verse, referencing each, and often preserving exact phrases and diction. Section three allows "an anon narrator" to express a People's History perspective, given the latitude of a blue-collar, working man's voice. In these three separate ways, the poems delve into the personal and socio-political issues experienced by the members of the Lewis and Clark Expedition, during that formative phase at Camp Dubois, prior to their official departure on May 14, 1804.

Concerns for the natural environment evidence themselves in these poems, and this, too, seems historically appropriate. For, as directed by President Thomas Jefferson, the map of the United States was being redrawn westward by the Lewis and Clark Expedition, premised upon Enlightenment Science and the economic and political objectives of an expanding Nation. The Expedition was motivated by a great cultural curiosity, as well as the desire for new lands and increased prosperity. The journals were meant to record these exploratory efforts and discoveries for the public, from what was termed a "Purely Literary Expedition."

The Journals of the Lewis & Clark Expedition remain as artifact to our national intents and purposes, and characterize us as a People, exemplified by the members and by those they met along the way. This history becomes a mirror for the contemporary world, allowing us an opportunity to perceive and examine cultural assumptions and values that have defined us as a Nation, for surely they contend within us, still, today.

To me, as author, there is nothing more important than a thoughtful and sensitive reader, with an active and critical mind, joining in this spirited conversation.

Mark B. Hamilton

September 7, 2025
Richmond, Indiana

A Tribute to the Romantics

Ode to Absence

i.

The oak has fallen in its slow slur of loss
across the empty air, the breadth of branches
gone, a weathered bell now tolling chaos.
Its fall has urged us all to take our chances
to redo the undone, to bridge this newest void
—this abyss once channeled by the stars.
Deciphered, their tangled images do fade
from substance to idea, although we avoid
believing warmth was hidden in that shade.
Our memories are built by tracing the scars,
the heart conflicted by what harm conspires.
Those unattended slights can fuel many fires.

ii.

As swirling sparks encircle a failing star,
the world beyond the wall has awoken
to pronounce each word as God from afar
while eastern skies approach as fires stolen.
A herd of deer approaches, grazing below,
their gracefully bent necks nibbling at food,
absorbing life from those unburnt shadows.
Our gnarled hands are both numb and crude,
our fingers unfurling in flame and bluster,
each log depleting the identity of the cutter.
Consumed by need, the uncensored fear
detaches from nature, and we, too, disappear.

iii.

Perhaps, Reason itself was the cutter of wood,
the axe, the saw that makes a future heavy.
From beneath our feet where nature had stood
we cut down the oak and felt ourselves worthy
of Nature's bounties as if they were a sign
for making changes to many other places.
The walnut, maple, spruce, hickory, and pine,

from landscapes we clear-cut by design,
have fallen as profits to warm a new Nation,
the children chasing winter's wild spaces
in answering one single, sacred question:
"What purpose holds their true destination?"

Upon Reading Scott's *The Common Wind*

i.

Every thought an idea. Each hope a vision.
From hazard to safety, from exploit to promise,
we celebrate freedom with the arisen
at Lent in maroon towns of the master less,
across the river in St. Charles as the sower,
and renegade in accord with dissident slave,
or pariah and agitator of repressive authority.
What fortress ever built by wealth and power
and greed, could withstand this will to save
ourselves with words declaring equality?
For Saint-Domingue was in restive mutiny,
like us, to liberate its community.

ii.

What rights? And for whom are they lawful?
At what price comes the public tranquility?
Their decision not to work was a refusal
that provoked elites to burn Paine's effigy.
When a Spanish *credula* in Caracas
was embraced by slaves as they revolted,
the Customs Agents knew the importance
of controlling information. Rebels insulted
investors, who had supported the elite politic,
but sailors denied "Many should profit the few,"
insisting instead that justice was a basic
truth established by a multi-lingual crew.

iii.

Beware when the slogan "Live Free or Die"
is altered to "Nation, Law, and King."
The economic hierarchy is the lie
that makes our lives a profitable thing.
Listen to the islanders in the Caribbean,
enraged and rising-up with insolence
untenable to the ears of Napoleon—

while slaves created at great expense
to France an independent Nation.
The economic elite lost profits in coffee,
sugar and rum, when replaced by liberation
and no longer able to rule by decree.

iv.

So we landed at village quays to trade
on market days and at local horse races
these worldly goods to a river of faces.
All intangibles into tangibles made.
A sleight-of-hand hidden in the fold,
made public with pamphlets we sold
and by symbols on trinkets and jewelry.
The Tricolor Cockade and Liberty Tree
etched by sailor and slave—an alteration
of time well-spent, expressing outrage
—their opinions so dangerously strange
they fostered Saint-Domingue's revolution.[i]

Ode to Causes

i.

Beneath a gibbous moon, the breathing mind
  imagines the slashing of a bright meadow
in winter's wilding haste. The north wind
  has clawed the limbs moving across the snow
like spiked armaments, perceived as the enemy
  conspiring with fear and fatigue to effect
our eyes and ears, as they widen to search
  the drifts with all five senses, altering a tree
into a threat until the dawn connects
  the earth to smoke and ends our long dogwatch.
From those labored hours, isolated in the cold,
  we revive the warmth we have controlled.

ii.

When sweet trees harbor the frozen sap,
  we sneak off to country stands for whiskey.
Like children hiding to avoid the strap,
  we claim our inherited freedoms early.
One has a plan to steal a horse, for women
  and gambling at Cahokia taverns,
to trade the hides we have for what he wants.
  Without a leader, one's personal opinion
distills into greed, and what he learns
  encourages his admiring vagrants.
While winter pronounces every name,
  the cold winds treat us all the same.

iii.

Our labor once honored existence, the senses
  absorbing every action the body could abide.
Exertions brought thirst that water quenches
  our work releasing a truth from the inside.
But punishment by the whip broke the skin
  into pain. Like sand gouged-out by a river,
the loss was recorded deeply within things.

A body regained its rightful intuition,
but the healing mind could never sever
those thoughts from hurt that damage brings.
Emotions bound the body, freed from above.
The scars were left between hate and love.

iv.

A deer hide gets tuckered to fit, then stitched.
The trees have sung our names. As tailor, smithy,
or thatcher, we are wild horses hitched
to sparks traveling upwards in the sky,
emotions kindling the steering, as a compass
cannot. When visions blur, the stars are fixed
with reasons why music carried and sugar healed.
We complete each task, with no frets to pass
inspections, and drink the corn mash mixed
to smother our reflections. Ready for the field,
we move within this moveable feast.
We stay inside the wondering beast.

An Oral History of the Mammoth in North America

—as told to Thomas Jefferson by a chief orator of the Delaware Nation, circa 1779

i.

He stood as if in celebration, a Delaware warrior in regalia:
the buckskin leggings and breechcloth panels, a colorful shirt
and tapered scarf, the deer skin moccasins and a bear skin turban,
all intricately beaded with strong designs of purple and white
in geometric and floral patterns. Over a shoulder, across his chest,
a wide band was attached to a paneled pouch slung at the hip,
ornamented with black turkey beard and two red-dyed deer tails.

He gestured with a fan of golden eagle feathers toward the floor,
then up into the heights of the room, as if striking the war post
to begin his oration, bold and melodious:

"Ten thousand moons ago when naught but gloomy forests
covered this land of the sleeping Sun, long before the pale man
with thunder and fire at his command rushed on the wings of wind
to ruin this garden of nature—when naught but the untamed
wanderers of the woods, and men as unrestrained as they,
were lords of the soil—a race of animals were in being,
huge as the frowning Precipice, cruel as the bloody Panther,
swift as the descending Eagle, as terrible as the Angel of Night.

"The Pines crashed beneath their feet; and the Lake shrunk
when they slacked their thirst; the forceful Javelin in vain
was hurled, and the barbed arrow fell harmless at their side.
Forests were laid waste at a meal, the groans of expiring Animals
were everywhere heard; and whole Villages, inhabited by men,
were destroyed in a moment—the cry of universal distress
extending even to the region of Place in the West.

"But the Good Spirit interposed to save the unhappy.
Forked lightning gleamed and loudest Thunder rocked the Globe.
Bolts of Heaven were hurled upon the cruel destroyers alone,
and the mountains echoed with their bellowing death.

"All were killed except one male, the fiercest of the race,
and him even the artillery of the skies assailed in vain,
as he ascended the bluest summit which shades the source
of the Monongahela, and roaring aloud, he bid defiance
to every vengeance."[ii]

ii.

We retired to the library,
a fire warming us, the candlelight flickering
the flames like the feathers of a scissortail. All of us
now as restful as the gentle, unbroken ancients.

Governor Jefferson, our kind host, then brought out
giant femurs and two large molars of an elephant
thought to inhabit still the far regions of the north.

Time seemed lost in that moment, as I remember,
gathering as we did in the shadowy realm of imaginings
to unroll a mostly blank map across a wide table.

Such was my evening with the Ordinary People,[iii]
the Lenape, our struggling friends and allies, like us
rebels in Virginia at war with the British.

From the Winter Journals of Captain William Clark

Shelter

> *"...fixed on a place to build huts Set the men to Clearing land & Cutting logs— a hard wind all day—flying Clouds, Sent to the neighborhood, Some Indians pass."*
> *—Captain Clark, Camp Dubois, December 13, 1803*

For huts the men must wield and bend
with slashing arms in worsening wind
the axes, trimming logs at both ends.
The geese that honk above remind
us all that time can be our failing,
so we tightly grip those flexing minds
of polished hickory handles. Each felling
that whips the air and crashes past could
kill with its weight of icy shimmering,
so we carefully clear the road that should
be cut a mile due east—as sharply blazed
in survey where I, Captain Clark, had stood.

The work results in a cabin raised
with fresh venison sizzling in the fire.
The others will take twelve more days
to cut and haul, and build the fort entire.
And though our every muscle aches
more food becomes the only desire,
the ashen coals left as ghostly lakes
from meals shared with Indians passing.

Our minds do doubt, but strength does take
that careful calculation for our waking.
When mornings offer just grouse in snow,
we listen for creaking wagons, hoping
for provisions from Cahokia tomorrow,
from Griffeth's farm or from traders we see
in pirogues with salt. Each day does bow
to night while fires smoke and seats empty,
the axmen and sawyers falling like trees
to sleep like logs, guarded by the sentry.[iv]

Under a Hazy Sun

Without the sun to lift this dreary weather, we
might lose our confidence in Nature—the faith
that hovers around a human body's frailty.

Before Mother Earth inspires spring, its wraith
of furrows will tow us through wending places
to guide the passing, as if a living breath.

With sweat that freezes, I recognize their faces,
these men who heft the logs into place. Their bold
hearts combine with every crafted brace.

In winter's numbing cold, they tightly hold
onto hope, and build the frames on solid hearths
from muddy wattle into a chimney scaffold.

These efforts might comprise our only worth,
these huts the tumbled columns of an ending
for this, their story does urge toward myth.

To those who seek its truth by the telling
a squared and plumbed measurement does matter
and has value, as pleasure expressed in the doing.

At noon I write, and Floyd arrives with a letter
from Lewis who supports McFarland's intention
of claiming expenses justly incurred, after

sustaining troops during the Whiskey Rebellion.
I walk up the hill for a meridian with sextant,
for a latitude of the camp under a hazy sun.

Then, I order Shields and Floyd out to hunt
for turkeys roosting above in a thickening sleet.
The keelboat needs adjustment of stores in front,

so we wade hip-deep in ice floes on freezing feet
to carry barrels ashore and stack under guard,
pounding the loose *pries* with mallets to reseat.

The Boat keeps tilting farther and harder aground,
yet there is nothing more we can do or replace.
The frosty mist hinders our work and has slowed

even the chimney builders, so I have them place
two Commissary horses for taking the load
off men's shoulders, dragging the logs in traces.

With teams, the hauling men now stride the road
enthused with new and more hopeful emotions.
This happy alteration has changed their mode

of work, diminishing their fear and predilection
that Old Hermit Winter might not care to sire
a sapling's leaf, preferring to keep them frozen.

With more horses and eight more men, Drewyer
returns, although none of them are in readiness.
They stand idle, seemingly without the desire,

like a wall of legs without apparent worthiness.
I send for another team of horses, and for corn
and turnips from Griffeth's farm, when a witness

from past campaigns does visit me this morn—
a Delaware Chief from the Greenfield Treaty
which ceded much land. His greeting has sworn

a remembrance of me, so I offer him whiskey,
which he declares is good. For today, at best,
the welcoming stays the raw weather, as we
shelter in huts with his Indian words, and rest.

Fresh Venison

A boon! The hunters hang the air with deer
swinging frozen, recovered by the blind fetch
made easy, since far off it's crows we hear
around those heaps of guts in a snowy ditch,
like a wallow of blood. While Drewyer again
hangs three more, plus turkeys at the fork,
a fourth is added by his Indian. The other men,
who lately arrived, have now begun to work—
to set a roof upon their hut without more loss
of my good opinion, which does mend. To folks
in the country, I send Shields paddling across
for butter, where he does well to avoid a soak
from pirogues trading south toward St. Louis.
A Frenchman, stops to visit, and confides in me
that several good voyageurs wish to join us,
as *engages* who know well the lower Missouri,
but he holds a strong concern for retaliation
from the Spanish Commandant, as that authority
remains absolute. I talk of our new possession
of Upper Louisiana, promising to pay a fee
for their knowledge, come spring to the Ocean.[vi]

December 25th

The Party stands at parade
with Stars and Bars above our fort.
A volley celebrates the completion
of shelters with its sharp report.

As leader, I honor the men
giving them two half-days,
plus full rations of whiskey
dismissed with three Hurrahs.

Most will frolic and drink a bit
in preparation for tonight—
the best of hunters trudging out
for turkeys in the misty light.

As always, there is some scuffling
to those finer points of youth—
their playful rough-house fights
resulting in a loosened tooth.

Others make fun until the strain
does lean one man to poke
the laughing face that's smiling
until he is seated on the joke.

But talk remains a goodly chore
that best satisfies the wrong—
before another head gets busted,
the learning don't take long.

A real problem does arise
when some who voice a side
don't have the brains enough
up there to cure a hide.

But mostly, they share and tussle
between the antlers and the hoof.
Some place a blame, but no one
really can find a proof.[vii]

A Gathering

John Shields returns with butter.
To Indians who Christmas with us,
we offer rations of whiskey
as hosts, and share our surplus.

Sergeant Ordway bawls them in
from work and wanderings, to retire
with sweat, but happy to sit on logs
so near the food and fire.

Amid our leathered shoulders
Drewyer interprets a message
into English of Nations east
who plan on attacking the Osage.

As Captain, I make explanation
to causes of our Government
in hopes that strong words now
will dispel their warring intent.

Displaced always farther west
the tribes do jostle and flee
from axes and towns, in the breach
of their desperate diplomacy.[viii]

The Feast

Drewyer will return to Massac,
but rejoin at the offered rate
as hunter and talker. A good load
like a wagon he carries the freight.

We might get hungry for awhile
as most of this Christmas meat
has been from the brain of his rifle
with which no other can compete.

Around the fires aglow at mess
each man has ample, plus some.
Bellies are full, the night is clear,
and all the stragglers are home.

At the bonfire we collect
the Indians and French among
our Party to celebrate the feast
with drum and fife and song

in Delaware and Canadian,
in Kickapoo and bottled cork,
a lyrical tune, a sounding horn,
a whistle and a flute, with York,

my slave, amid the fancy ankles,
and everyone crowding-in
for turkeys turning on the spits
with sticks of sizzling venison.

They drink the proffered gills
with pleasure warming their feet,
while I remain in shadow,
my hut and chimney complete.

Every softened hide is claimed
for clothing and high moccasins.
Even feathers are divvied up
for bunks to stuff with padding.

Their quickened spirits flash in fun.
A tambourine of stretched rabbit
is struck and thumped as if unhinged
from bones of that Old Hermit.

With fiddles, song, and laughter
they forget all thoughts of sorrow,
and feast into the offered dark
to stay awhile for tomorrow.[ix]

Work Days

Four details under command,
sentries posted and hidden
near fellers, haulers, and carpenters,
protecting the wattling men.

A pine slashes the morning breeze.
The day's work begins
with the warming breath of gills
poured now-and-again.

Those who favor chunking wood
have their own hand-hewn tools
in constant motion worn to smooth.
A few lazy ones do act the fools.

Two hide buckets full of mud,
leaves and twigs for wattle,
one man inside, one man out,
both chinking on one bottle.

Logs get notched and placed,
the oxen shake their coats,
goods and blankets drying out
as Floyd tallies up the Boat.

Willard and Roberson return
with letters from St. Louis,
sharing news of wooden walks
and women sightings to remind us.

They help to stow the heavy stores
neatly in good order, amusing us all
with stories of excess, and laughing
while stretching them up real tall.

The ice builds. We caulk and trim.
Whitehouse and York apace—
two sawyers with a saw that sings
back-and-forth in place.

Winds do give, then take away
that bee-sweet scent of resin.
In seasoned arms a tug-of-war
between them both can win.

To repeat a task is never easy.
To relax one's strength until
the calming frees a bind—a pace
is best that ends in skill.[x]

The Paddlers and the Swan

—a fabliau by an anon narrator

The one in front reaches far out
for wings in a blur and a flurry.
A jug or two has passed between,
no doubt. The fun is in the hurry.

Six hands are clenched to guide.
Their knees are bent and ready
to clamor after God's own truth
in kind the true, and … steady.

They sit atop a wooden ditch
as if they were a'stradle
behind a horse's lathered mouth
the strength, purpose, the saddle.

They go much faster than is fast
sitting sidled in the middle,
each paddle tip a stirrup
on gallop over a muddy puddle.

The flurry of all six arms
a'flying both sides of that swan
increases the goodly humor
with more whiskey in early dawn.

Our jokes become sworn epithets:
"Napoleon! We'll stay your hope!
When Frogs can catch our dinner
we'll celebrate with the Pope!"

All four hearts are pounding strong.
They caught it with a final thud!
2 miles below, like Lafayette
and soaked in Mississippi mud.

A succulent meal of freedom
renewed, renewed in deed.
For all the blessings of Nature
a silent throat, a fluted reed.

The swan now for the griddle
clapped away by those on board
in hopes of owning everything—
a good fire, and the Lord.

Their hunger chased that terror,
its shattered brilliance of white
across the muddy flat of water
two wings in fearful flight.

And O! how a priestly smock
does hide the night that sings
of robed angels who must flock
to each, this bone mill of wings.[xi]

So Ends the Year

In my snug and completed hut
I write to my Julia's father.

On snowy fields Drewyer kills
one deer, and his Indian another.

I think of Virginia, the fallen snows,
and my brother-in-law in Kentucky

on this bright and balmy day
with a purity settling around me.

I order two most trusted men
to Cahokia with this letter.

Colter brings in deer and turkey.
In passing years, I will miss her.[xii]

The Market Place, 1804

The wind does cry in empty circles
around a cold and flickering lamp.
In snowy steps a woman wishes
to wash and mend for all in camp.
She walks amid the Detachment,
interacts and draws her presence
toward fires whose warmth has meant
our comfort, and now her reliance.

To trade, the neighbors bring sugar,
and rifles to shot at the mark.
I purchase 6 pounds and put up a dollar—
the best of two to win the bark.
I pace the target. Gibson is best,
but country folks win the dollar.
A bargain gets struck to sew a vest
to stay the cold with its fur collar.

As Reed and Wiser drink a truce,
the produce seller tells us, "I cuts
these from marshes, a yellow lotus
I pull and dry, and call pond-nuts."
The day becomes a market place
exchanging goods and information:
one man, a blacksmith, can retrace
his visit north to the Mandan Nation.

A fattened pig is brought to barter
for hides or a useful tin item,
or coinage from the bag. Then later
all is merry as whiskey is the custom.
At Cahokia, Captain Lewis will remain
on business important to the enterprise,
while a veteran from King's Mountain
does visit, named Captain Whitesides.

He brings his son with all the urges
to join the Expedition. In youthful
vigor, ambitious to be tried, he purges
my prodding, like a careful bull.[xiii]

Establishing Order

Blustery and 21 below—
the wind blowing sand into a fury
that darkens this day to make it so
dreadful gusts siphon the Missouri.

The sky does split thickly swirled
branches, cutting open the arbors
that blanket our accustomed world,
the men bending to their labors.

Some members drink, others fight,
as I continue to evaluate the men.
The few blackguards I hold in sight
I'll weed from my human garden.

Some are better shots than others,
and will be the expert marksmen
to best use these rifled calibers
for grizzly and threats from Indians.

Corporal Robinson, the posted leader
when the Sergeant was away,
allowed privates Potts and Warner
to leave their hut at night, to display

their dislike of one another, the cause
of much bruising without authority.
Yet most others, even with their flaws,
have stayed fairly merry in company.

28 boatmen will be necessary:
2 Captains, the rowers, York, 4 extra,
and 2 interpreters. Not a bowery,
nor a bag of worms. Not a Medusa.

Of the forty total, three will be sick.
A weakness always within. The Boat
and two pirogues are hard and thick,
like shields to form an effective moat.

6 soldiers in the white pirogue,
7 engages in the red, will defend
in teams of competing rogues,
as flankers holding the bitter end.

At parade, I speak on previous orders,
reviewing tabulations of their actions
from my field notes kept of members,
for each a name with any infractions.

I order those who had then fought,
got drunk, or neglected their Duty,
to remain at post until they brought
enough wood to build hut and chimney

for the resolute woman who promised
to wash and sew for the Detachment.
Completed under guard, I dismissed
them with cautions to their Sergeant.[xiv]

Cold Work

The Mississippi is frozen
with ice stacked on both sides.
The Dubois River banks cave-in
as we reset the weakened pries.

At night, we work in sleet and rain
on slippery mud in hip-deep water
to lift the Boat as shores loosen.
Yet pride holds, and we do not falter.

The hunters, I sent out for grouse,
report that half a hog was found
as bear bait hanging, swinging loose.
No signs of an owner, but still sound.

Shields will ask the neighborhood
whose hog it was, as bad weather tries
us all till midnight, the strong and good
struggling to right and fix the pries.

After drying out, I find an opportunity
to draw, while my servant tends the fire.
I map the Platte above Osage territory,
further realizing the worth of Drewyer,

who has departed to settle his affairs.
Although replaced by Colter and Shannon,
the hunt of creek and prairie for bears
diminishes our food to the common.

I postpone the afternoon inquiry,
when Fields shoots another deer today,
and as my anger rises. On the Mississippi
more liquor is being sold by Ramey.

The sawyers, Whitehouse and Reed
have improved together with the logs,
and Shields says a family, who traded
onions for tin, complained of a lost hog.

Abandoned in ruins yet standing still
the old French fort remains opposite.
Salt works get built at each grist mill
in clearings of every new town site.[xv]

Ancient Mounds

Collins had found the hog, butchered and hung,
so we left early that morning with our rifles slung
to hunt the prairie fowl with shot, and to explore
Dubois River, hoping our slow and stealthy tour
might surprise a bear at dinner. Approaching near
we fell into a stalk beneath a rise, only to hear
loud caws from the carcass, speckled with crows
having devoured the meat to bones. Above the snow
all was ears, a mask attached to a spine, the thin
shadow of a corpse hanging in the wind to spin
its yarn of dying for some hungry farmer's larder.
So we kept the hunt southeastward, a bit farther
from the bottoms, where we spotted prairie fowl
on roosting branches, like silhouettes of owl.
We fired one-by-one taking several and more
at the foot of berry bushes, until we both wore
the grouse as Indians might wear feathered capes.
Continuing our trek toward some distant shapes
we imagined to be a group of ancient mounds,
an expanse in front was wide and not a sound
was heard as we approached in this field of fire.
Without the ice underfoot an attack would mire
and deepen quickly into failure, yet we strode in
across that level surface of the pond, frozen
enough to get us committed far into the middle.
Until at 100 yards, all broke loose into a riddle
of children singing "little piggy's," in the moat
up to our chests, rifles held high, unable to shoot.
The ancients knew well a defense against infantry
building on ground to weaken the attacking enemy.
So we backed out, returning far around to the south
amid the prairie stubble, keeping out of the mouth
of that big frog, and approached the fortification
of 9 mounds in a round—a haven of protection,
an Indian fortress once encircled by palisades
with whistling wings of two more mounds made
7 feet above the prairie. All scattered with flint
and earthen ware. An entire high and dry settlement
below the sky, while northward an immense grave,

with a Cahokia woodhenge, had been built to save
their loved ones by the sacred motion of the sun.
Returning at sunset, I found my feet well frozen
inside my shoes. My slave rubbed them with snow
and wrapped them both, setting them gently low
on the hearth, slowly, to prevent the frost bite.
With westerly winds exceedingly cold that night
York brought firewood and plucked two hens.
"This 'ill help, Massa. With good luck, and then
hot broth and God ta' thaw out your feet again."[xvi]

Unwell

In sheets, the ice moves the dark.
I am unwell from my recent dunking.
J. Fields returned after some risk
of paddling across that flowing,

to report that people greatly favor
recent surveys by Captain Mackay
of granted lands that do comprise
a beautiful and bountiful country.

Indisposed, I remain quite sick.
McNeal and Ordway lost all night,
the Missouri impassable with ice,
like shuffling cards, a forceful sight.

My servant keeps the fire so hot
the chimney wattle catches aflame,
so I take the meridian at noon
as others douse the burning frame.

The rivers are rising, and Pryor
arrives from Cahokia with letters,
the Boat afloat, in perfect order.
Though sleeping little, I am better.

With evening rains, dry and tight
in huts, we cook rabbits at mess,
the Mississippi stoppered with ice,
the bubbling stew a great success.[xvii]

Winter was Deep

—for Jon Carlson, USACE, Ret. by an anon narrator

In drifting snows from the west
morning brings along the creek
a crunching to our smoky fire—
the horses' hooves in early hour.

We crouch above the chunks of wood
inhaling ashes, the night was so cold
it broke the silence from our voices
into songs to calm those anxieties.

We wondered, were wondering still
until the woods awoke. Then I
and 7 other men rushed out to tarry
with the long truant commissary.

We put our shoulders to his gate
pushing through the broken ice to get
the rations expected from his contents
reserved solely for our Detachment.

He dippered-out the traded whiskey.
Our frozen feet crunching on ice
as we followed quickly with our arms
out-stretched for those offered alms.

Entering camp slightly winded,
but aware of our arrival, we continued
sipping tin cups with lip and tongue
bellied-up to the end of his wagon.

The winter was deep in rousing scenes
with all the men surrounding, the steam
of horses straining tack, the smack
of teeth on cups cradled from the back.

A gill for every man who spoke
for Major Rumsey, who opened trunks
to trade with permissions granted
for skins and hides our work provided.

Then, we shot for a pair of *leagens*,
competing with country folk. Field given
the best, then Winser, Shields, and Frazer,
as every goodly shot we did remember.

After Gibson, Colter, and Pryor
returned with letters and newspapers,
and metal bits and files to sharpen,
the sober work did commence again.

The ice, 20 yards from shore,
was one fist thick. Gibson killed more
deer, Colter 3 turkey, and Shields 4,
14 rabbits from Thompson and Warner.

The winter was deep. Our huts solid.
The Sergeant's mess sang a ballad.
Some sewed sinew, some trimmed lead,
joining in rounds, all were well fed.[xviii]

Plans for Spring

The Mississippi breaks its swollen moat
into floes so strong they shuffle up the bank
arousing thoughts, both strange and remote.

In fog, the grouse are easy game, roosting hens,
and Hall has bagged many rabbits with snares,
but still, it is meager fare for forty men.

While York cooks a stew, I estimate the voyage
westward, then north and west again, to my extent
of knowledge, the mountains but a short portage.

An optimism recurs with thoughts of summer,
the Mandan, the ocean's tide to follow spring,
returning to St. Louis by next December.

The Boat, a nameless galley, needs 20 rowers
to pole and cord, ascending the mighty Missouri
at barricaded stations hinged with covers.

I measure for boards and sketch examples of pins,
make lists of materials for sawyers and blacksmiths.
The Permanent Party must be men of discipline.

Captain Lewis and I will establish martial rule
as directed by the articles of war. In abidance, each
to understand that punishments could be painful.

An aft cabin will be built with ridgepoles head high
for taut awnings over helmsmen and blunderbuss,
the mast on a tabernacle lowered when limbs defy.[xix]

Sick in Bright Light

For days in heavy snows the rivers run with slushy ice.
In north winds, we stay in huts eating deer and rabbits.
I am weak and very unwell, and take Dr. Rush's physics.

Last night was very cold. The branches, gilded with ice,
are magnificent with frost. Yet I am sick, and do not sleep.
The sunrise was clear and beautiful, the blue sky so deep.

While mantled in smoke, rivers flow below the misty ice.
Gibson kills 2 deer. Others raccoons and rabbits in quantity.
I order sleighs to be built for hauling wood from the country.

The freezing snows accumulate. Men break through the ice.
Another sled is built for firewood, and stores get weighed.
The kegs of pork and flour, whiskey, and corn are measured,

then stowed in the Boat, leaning on pries in the shifting ice.
Winser was out all night. I am unwell. Although some better,
I send Howard express to Capt. Lewis with an urgent letter.

Consumed with cracks, the river crunches its shingling ice.
Winser returns with turkey and deer. R. Field, Gibson,
and Collins another. Heat and food become our reason.[xx]

Potatoes, Brandy and Porter

—an anon narrator

Last night, all the porter froze
and several other bottles broke.
The men now stack them exposed
to thaw—a bitter beer that folk
favor as brewed from charred malt.
Quite good with apples and salt.

Visitors arrive with warming skies.
3 Frenchmen from Portage des Sioux
with potatoes, fowl, meal and brandies,
and women who sell breads, and sew.
The scene widens as the trading grows,
exchanges becoming people we know.

The Captain delivers new canisters
of powder, while walking up the hill
with sextant, giving flints to hunters
and swinging the sun's image until,
reflected in a mirror, it sits so lined
the horizon is more precisely defined.

He writes the position and calculates
by time, as drawn from tables in a book
of the instrument's angle, which takes
in plenty of columns when we look.
But we depart before he commences.
We go outside to replenish our senses.

The sun always shows us where we are.
It rises without the need for a bobble
with fine brass knobs that measure so far
a steed only Captain Clark can hobble.
Later, from Cahokia the mails arrive,
Captain Lewis saying that he will strive

to be at camp tomorrow. There being
more letters from Kentucky, eight cork
bottles of wine, and files for sharpening,

Sergeant Ordway orders us back to work.
Captain Clark has received a soft, tough
Durant, a woolen cloth to wrap his cough.[xxi]

Visions North

I sent the best of my hunters out
in twos upriver. Then, about
sunset Lewis arrives with riders:
accompanied by Mister Hay,
an Indian merchant, fur trader,
and postmaster of Cahokia,
who offers us a rare copy
of the Mackay-Evans' journal
from travels, which they convey
as discoveries in informal
terms of the upper Missouri River;
and Mister Jo Hays, the sheriff
of Cahokia, to protect and deliver
this item, so worthy of our belief.

The deer are slung on horseback
when shot at separate cross-tracks,
these five to feed our inventory,
plus Reed's wild cat killed in thick
brush along the creek. Yet the worry
that I continue to be very sick,
as my head aches much, does hurry
Captain Lewis. Come early morning,
we travel quickly beneath a canopy
of gilded ice to the planned meeting
with Mr. Catlett, a surgeon's mate
from Captain Stoddard's artillery.
Along the sharp river rocks, my fate
approaches slowly towards me.[xxii]

Still Very Unwell

It is warming, but I am unwell this mile
in the cold and frost, on Mister Hays' horse
accompanying the gentlemen for a while
for their departure, yet I am feeling worse.

The thaw is fair. High winds have increased.
I take more medicine, remaining sick all day.
To Leakens, a thief who must be discharged
from our Party, I give a small correction of pay.

The curving wings of fowl pass briefly overhead,
and I remain unwell. Dubois River is fastly rising,
lifting the Boat off its pries, and in stead
refloating it up-creek, although today is warming.

A straight line must inhabit those feathery brains.
My servant tends and feeds the fire, and Mr. Hanley
sends butter and milk in a wagon of Mr. Koehn's,
whose wife asks how she might better comfort me.

Those wild, gliding wings are the soul. I am sick.
Captain Lewis sends out Shields for walnut bark.
Winser kills a badger, the ice is 11 inches thick.
The river has washed away its water mark.

A whistling swan flies above whispering a dream.
The walnut pills have taken effect, and I feel better.
A Maumee canoe drifts away, lost downstream,
and news gets delivered by Mr. Hay's messenger

with invitations to attend the Balls at St. Louis.
The Missouri keeps spewing a slushy reef
of muddy floes that form its half-frozen surface,
the geese and swans afloat in a marshy sheaf.[xxiii]

People's History at River Dubois
by an Anon Narrator

Captain Clark is Very Sick

Our Captain had developed the deep pleurisy,
becoming sick and bed-ridden with its toll,
so weak with cough Captain Lewis brought
a surgeon's mate from Stoddard's artillery.
Encamped due south, as ordered they sought
a transfer of Louisiana to American control.

Experience must now guide us to maintain
the pace that Captain Clark had set. The worst
fear makes his frailness our own—a lesson
that each of us owes, as he mounted his horse
with help from York—the sickness the reason
for his strength to go, with treatment uncertain.

Captain Lewis was in St. Louis on business
important to the enterprise, and had not been
at camp as leader, as it now stands well-built
with huts inside the palisades. Nor had he seen
the increasing weakness of Captain Clark, or felt
his struggle, which we found so hard to witness.

Attired for travel in leggings, newly cleaned,
his soft coat buckles well-shined and leathers
with straps and boots well-oiled, all glistening
like the fur of his dog, Captain Lewis leaned
forward to urge his horse into a cantering
up to its hocks through snow, dragging tethers.

Last night, we had bundled-up in wind and ice
for an evening parade, as the sunset had cast
its shadow from the palisade. Stiffly at attention
we stayed in silence, as if at Captain's mast,
to hear the Order removing Clark to St. Louis
for his necessary care and recuperation.

Shields was sent to search for a medical herb
by Captain Lewis, which added to our concern
for Captain Clark, for he had earned our loyalty.

As working men watchful of health, we labored
with fatigue and its possible companion injury,
under his guidance, so wished him a safe return.

Every man was proud of the fort, this shelter
poised like a Colonial hat, slightly cocked
in a "V," the 10 x 10 huts slanted with snow
as designed by Clark while at Wood River.
These huts were built with logs, four in a row,
"Impervious to cannon balls," he had joked.

The storehouse between had a platform above,
a lookout for the Boat and an all-day sentry.
The palisades allowed a gate to the road
due east, through the woods as the sun moves,
for timber, oaken planks, and firewood towed
by horse teams rented from folks in the country.

Our quarters were snug, but our Captain was ill.
He needed treatment for his worsening condition.
Captain Lewis would return in two-days-time
once Captain Clark was settled and the mission
complete. Our Sergeant would command until
then, with all of us making best use of the time.

A wet winter wind froze the air as if a burden,
but we kept composed and held to silent spaces
until dismissed to mess from that evening's parade.
Some talked of sickness, some the threat and sudden
surprise of death. Others had tightly braised faces
gazing at the fire, noticing a few gestures made.

We knew the grumblings betrayed uncertainty
to our sense of who, what, and where. So many
would just stay the course no matter the why.
Concerned and committed as army enlistees,
we slept in the darkened sounds of a muted sky
like fiery logs drowsing into smoky hickory.

Two Days Without

i.

The bear-like dog was drawn along, to lope
across on the icy crust, as Captain Lewis
astride his horse beneath an arching wood
took Clark in tow. While hunching forward
his servant followed amid tilted slabs of snow
—their silhouettes aflame in the ragged light
like remnants of cloth torn from the rising sun.

The Sergeant shouted assignments at parade
for work details and guard duty, dismissing us
to eat a corn porridge at mess. In groups, we
gathered quickly, warming to the tasks, wishing
Captain Clark renewed health and success.
Our leader was well-versed in wilderness life
and knew the strife of long winter campaigns,
—those wearied dangers at isolated outposts
low on stores and threatened by loneliness—
those hungers that drove a man in raw weather
to find solace in fighting, whiskey, and sleep.

No wonder the sounds of clinking draft animals
were calming. Their bells, shanks, breath and bits,
the dragging chains from skids pulling a sled
that squeaked and slid and crushed the dry snow
created a peace of mind beyond the drudgery.
From chore to chore, we walked behind policing
the camp, then down to break the ice for water
with axes hefted above a drowsy, foggy river,
filling wooden barrels we topped-off for troughs
placed along the interwoven paths of army life.

And often we found contentment in the quietude
of falling snow that veiled a hunter's readied rifle,
concealing the scent of a body's rising breath,
while others set goods and bedding out to dry
or scrubbed the cook's black kettle. Everyone

had dug the trench, lugged the ashes, or stood
an early watch as sentry for horses and sawyers
who felt their sweat in spite of freezing weather,
as muscles ached, shoulders swayed, and hands
cramped around the tools that gave us a name.

ii.

Imagine how this rough-cut world could turn
toward far away thoughts of luxuriant ease,
where village lambs encouraged the spring
by lolling on rolling hills as skies unfold.
With festive dancers wrapped in the joyously
shining warmth, and scented orange candles
surrounding fresh baked bread. In musical tunes
inside our oaken room, a stone and walnut floor
gleamed with the colorful shoes beneath gowns
that swayed on its fluid gaiety, past porticoes
of moon-lit symphonies, and verandas enraptured
by carriages arriving and by servants floating
platters of gifts for the regal passengers
assisted up the steps of newly swept snow.

How we could envision those elegant Gala Balls
with their republican jackets and liberty gowns,
with voices of women conversing in perfumes
along tables sumptuously strewn with fresh game
and roasted pork, rare beef, and French pastries.
A world so bountiful with the spacious rustling,
so free to waltz around the room in strong arms
of brightly attired officers, as we, the hesitant
in our frippery of shadow, listened to laughter
and the teasing promises of hosting elites
as happy portents for their most gracious ladies.

By day we used our strength, honing our skills
as teamster, carpenter, picket, or clerk, and worked
together through the early hoof-hours. But at night,
we escaped the loneliness at country stands

to sit and drink their harsh cider and rum
as blacksmith or blackguard, no matter. We held
ourselves apart and within, and were rowdy until
on wooden racks in huts and smoky-drenched,
we awoke for morning parade, a bit groggy.

Camp & Mess

The palisades of pine would cast their shade
inside the fort, until the sun had risen
to form a space of heated mud that made
the work unpleasant. In short, it was an oven.
Our constant endless chores caused little pride,
the continual supervision an irritation,
unless scrubbing a kettle or stretching a hide
was one's cherished idea of an army ambition.
Yet every day, a lucky man was reassigned
to work outside the gate. His replacement
would grouse, argue and bray, only to find
that barracks duty was not a personal affront.
The work was for the common good and central
to our health—as necessary as salting a barrel.

Stores & Supply

Floyd was soft spoken and kept the stores.
He supplied the rations, and also acted
as *aide-de-camp*, following strict orders.
He was trusted and reliable, and conducted
the distributions with an integrity of habit.
The Party could eat a herd of deer, or pounds
of meal with sap, and each a warren of rabbit.
A tool from Floyd would be sharp and sound.
At night, when the huts filled-up with smoke,
we would strategize over mess with laughter,
and jostle a bit with jokes that might provoke
a few tense moments better left for after.
But Floyd steadied us, with his daily renewal,
reminding us that a future was useful.

Hunters

The magic, myth, and mystery are fine.
A hunter stays in tune with what is near.
The scented space that holds a quiet pine
can turn the slightest breeze to tempt a bear.
Our heightened senses embrace the soul.
The mind is freed by nature's tenderness.
As hunters, we enact, but do not control
the strength of will that determines success.
To snare a rabbit, or track and spot the buck
in sheltered apple, oak, or stream they frequent
is knowledge gained from them, not ego or luck.
The worthiness is patience mixed with scent.
Our palate tastes, our ears compare. We feel
the birthing heart, when earth is made real.[xxiv]

Sawyers

Nathaniel Pryor never shirked a task.
The difficult work was backbreaking.
He took his turn, and was not the one to ask
if pride as sawyer was worth contending.
Without York, the slave, others were chosen
in pairs to slant the arcing song of the saw—
to cut the planks for rowing seats and cabin,
completing Clark's requests without a flaw.
On platforms, the oak was wedged into place,
the blade in the slot from a ditch beneath,
a two-foot trunk making a six-cut surface.
In winter's shade, men caught their breath,
rewarded with extra gills of rum or whiskey.
And a sawyer was exempt from guard duty.

Blacksmiths

As craftsmen: Shields was master of tools. Willard,
a bit wayward with drink, but skilled and strong.
They punched-through hot metals hissing with hard
inner hearts of oak and burls billowing into song.
The iron curled and pins were peened, described
in Clark's memorandum. Every molten flange
was steeled in cold water and carefully designed
for planks that would stop a ball at close range.
Their projects required many special skills
to make, repair, and build. As valued gunsmiths
of rifles and muskets, they made things possible.
The forge held secrets in the steam like a myth,
when seats were hinged into barricades for safety,
transforming the Boat into a Missouri River Galley.

Sugar Makers

A sugar bush along the Dubois River
supplied syrup for corn porridge and coffee.
From gash to gouge, a trough would deliver
the sap to workers stirring sticks in a slurry.
One chopped, another carried. A useful limb
up-tilted buckets and granules were collected.
As thin sap thickened, temperatures did climb
in steaming kettles above fires carefully tended.
On Washington's Birthday trees slowly froze
and mud clung like fetters to shackle our feet
like slaves in Saint-Domingue. The sun rose
that day, but hasty puddings tasted less sweet.
A little winter bird flittered in a flurry.
The maple trees no longer in a hurry.

Voyageurs

The hired boatmen were French-Canadian,
Acadians from New Orleans, and Ottawa,
who wore bright sashes over blousy linen
and spoke in dialect with a strange *patois*—
as if a palisades around their brotherhood.
They laughed and sang communal commands
completing independent motions, and could
return at night to families without reprimands.
In time, we grew to admire these *engage*
who ate from sacks of pemmican and peas,
from Quebec, Montreal, and Chateauguay
with *dit* names, like *La Liberte* or *Jeunesse.*
At first, as soldiers, we did not comprehend
those river currents they would recommend.[xxv]

Captain Lewis Returns

Captain Lewis kept his promise
returning to inform us of his mission,
"Captain Clark is at Chouteau's mansion
recovering on Rue de Royale."

He settled into the Captain's quarters
at the southwestern prong of the "V"
with views of camp, platform and sentry,
his door open to the stepping guards

as posted, inside and out the gate.
When not observing a quarrel
he read field notes and the journal,
catching up on us, we thought.

To assist, Sergeant Ordway
would clarify a lengthy jotting
with subtle gestures or a dull nodding
above the stoop of his shoulders,

conveying back to us
the orders for our idling hands.
Captain Lewis's commands
were specific and impersonal.

Our skills, actions, and infractions
applied by his observations
determined work and duty stations,
transforming the camp's routine.

With Clark, we accomplished much
together with a common currency—
that practiced skill and fluency
in a craft, which was important to us.

But Lewis's leadership
had changed relationships to maintain
a precise military chain
of command that he insisted upon.

Reined-In

The Sergeant assigns
work details as ordered,
and forms us into lines.
Routines are managed
by the chain of command
the Captain has arranged.

At noon, we all stand
for one try at the target
at fifty paces off-hand.
The best marksman got
an extra gill of whiskey.
One man argues his shot.

A few dodge the Duty,
but most practice the drill.
While keeping the sentry
we stay focused until
we perfect von Steuben
as a practiced martial skill.

Some have become sullen.
The emotion is common.

von Steuben's Drill

Each night advised our attitude
in forming into ranks. The morning
river travels south with the sun
above the woods, our flag flying.

North winds are streaking snow;
we rub inside our coats;
the guard muffled against the cold;
the road is a whitening moat.

Captain Lewis departs today
for Gala Balls at St. Louis.
Sergeant Ordway will command
with Detachment Orders for us:

Duties specified day and night.
Compliance to rations of rum.
Work details rewarded a few,
seemingly unfair to some.

Plums were given that out-sized
soldiers as those quickly risen,
promoted to stations or proffered
freedoms to hunt by his decision.

The will was placed beyond our reach.
The ranks are measured by heights
centered outwards to higher ends
held by those with Corporal stripes.

Grouped in mass as marching wool
we tromp on bleating feet to say
that many think it wise to search
warily the watchful eyes of Ordway.

A shouted name corrects the line.
We keep on not asking the why,
plodding across on frozen ground
berating those who refuse to try.

A strong man became quite small
inside that commonly held gaze.
Every emotion was constrained
to be only what it conveys.

Scoffing was one such voice
a woodsman in rank could hear,
but soldiers usually accepted
orders without that sense of fear.

With sharp commands to go Left!
or Right! the nine pound muskets
were shouldered with a quick heft,
with long-spiked bayonets

a bristling thicket of muzzles
to threaten all others around.
If discipline from one foot undid
the oblique step, we all lost ground.

If someone splintered, veered-off
or wandered to the wrong side,
we'd wonder, "Where was he going?"
while lunging two and four-wide.

Directed by shouts, to the right,
to the left, to wheel or halt,
or face-about to where we came,
the cadence diminished fault.

Parades were one body, one mind,
that mirrored each other's skill.
Sergeant Ordway marched us
en masse to von Steuben's drill.[xxvi]

In Step with Burdens

The Kickapoo came in to talk,
"Our shadows have been broken
by your promises of heaven,
and chase us into the sunset."

Ladders lean against the roofs.
It is the Order of the Day
passed-on by Sergeant Ordway
to guards more strictly dressed.

No longer determined by choice
each step is stiff with discipline
as Sergeant, Corporal, or enlisted men
on a roster, in rotations kept.

The Duty makes it strenuous
and interferes with whisky runs,
to gamble items or sell the skins
on forays to country stands.

For the Sergeant of the Guard
the lengthening of morning parade
into formal inspections has made
"To arms!" an expectation.

Captain Lewis stations himself
at the flag pole in full uniform,
and judges our response to conform
to command with musket and rifle.

Tired, we stack them in a round—
a hardened stillness the distance
we leave in silent resistance
to those added hours of drill.

Captain Lewis Departs

—a shanty

Then, off he rode
with his dog on the road

through the winter snows
of Camp Dubois

back to Cahokia
and the Seven Taverns.

Then, off he rode
with his dog on the road

to the ferryman
crossing the Mississippi

to quays on the other side
with mansions on the hill.

Then, off he rode
with his dog on the road

into old St. Louis
along Rue de Royale

where Captain Clark was ill
at Chouteau's Corner.

Then, off he rode
with Captain Clark on the road

to attend the Gala Balls
with banquets without us.

Morning Muster

Our bodies strive for warmth and stay reserved
in actions defined by the heightening of the sun
as we move from fire to fire, policing the huts,
fetching tools and gear as guard or carpenter,
as axman or blacksmith. Then, mulling together
near the opened fort gate, we form into ranks
to buffet the winter wind streaming through.

Sgt. Ordway shouts our names from the roster,
and the Orders of the Day. We stand to attention,
the Duty given to pickets and tasks to work details,
and to Corporals who must remain vigilant
in marching the formation outside the palisades.

To others, who lack any special skill or craft,
the postings are often to more onerous chores,
like cleaning kettles, cutting tinder, or brimming
the barrels with freezing river water to haul,
while some split firewood and stack it in a pile
until it is higher than a hut. All this work requires
sweat and sometimes seems a punishment,
but it has to be done. Occasionally, everyone
had emptied the morning bucket into the trench
or caught the Duty like a dog in bad weather,
in thrashing winds at the most unpleasant hour.

But postings end the same with a break at noon
for marksmanship, which is our favored event.
Each man enjoys the precision of an exercise
in controlling the result exactly as expressed.
And the best receives an extra gill of whisky,
so efforts to load and ram, and aim do keep us
well-focused, and purposefully curious
to see who wins. Captain Lewis has limited
the fun, allowing only one shot to each,
but the fifty-calibers are sleek, and Ordway
has kept a strict account for every attempt.

The work day slips away, when marching back
to evening parade through a surrounding wood
that spills its warmth as the flag is lowered, folded
and stowed. Then, Sergeant Ordway dismisses us.
Our tired bodies, hungry and ready for mess,
have hopes for fatty meats, biscuits, and rum.
At night, we burrow into racks like chipmunks,
listening to the sentries pacing the cold dark.

Discipline Falls Abject

An army private stands to attention
while another sways the line with talk.
The Sergeant reflects their intention
then orders us into a rattling walk.

He commands by the Book, and keeps a tally
of actions and infractions, the Duty rotated fairly.

The flag is raised. The flag is lowered
in both sunrise and slanting shade.
A rifle or French musket is shouldered,
then charged, and aimed for the *enfilade.*

With heels apart, in precisely measured cadence,
a few refuse to obey, objecting with disobedience.

A colt will keep its body entire
confused by having a rider. No wonder
our Sergeant from New Hampshire
evokes their anger like thunder.

Their stormy eyes are untamed and shy of bridles.
They buck and buck and buck the cinching of saddles.

They refuse with disrespect
the Revolutionary von Steuben,
while others learn to accept
becoming better men.

Mostly, a blackguard will hide amid the Company,
but at times, enraged, he'll appear as the enemy.

When bayonets got mired
the risks got other men gored.
Close-quarter drills required
a precision not to be ignored.

At night, some men drank and some went absent.
Colter loaded a gun and threatened the Sergeant.

Warner, Potts, Collins, and Frazer,
Newman, Whitehouse, and Fields
all began riding their own anger
like Gibson, Colter, and Shields.

At morning muster, in dress uniform to inspect,
we performed the manual, but discipline fell abject.

Unsettled in huts, we find
no one who is truly at ease.
Many are solemn, deaf or blind,
while others try to appease.

Like a night bucket brimmed-up with ice, a faction
of men overflow with strife, and cause disruption.

The seven Cahokia taverns
remain just miles to the south,
and tempt the few with lanterns
refilled by an unruly mouth.

A mutiny would trek toward prison. All was distrust.
Our liberties were stretching across the frozen crust.

To Quell the Unrest

Captain Lewis returned to judge our conduct,
while inside the fort a blustery winter wind
has wrapped us in its icy stillness. We think
of little else but passing moments, working
on tasks as assigned. In this sullen atmosphere,
our grumblings become depressed and anxious,
distrustful and worried about the punishments
that might accompany his martial decision.
Unease is common among the men. A mutiny
remains possible, for many wish to escape
the harsh lashes from the unyielding whip.
Frontiersmen comprise much of the Company,
and are unused to the regulations soldiers obey.
Yet Captain Lewis takes testimonies as offered
in pros and cons, to conduct a fair inquiry
from men urged to speak in full confidence.
With gaunt expressions afterwards, their stress
and effort to achieve a clarity with honesty
reflects our hope for a rightful conclusion.
A few complain and keep drinking whiskey,
but to most it matters that order be restored,
as ultimately, our success depends upon it.

Abuse by Some

Abuse by some a detriment to most
with visits to whiskey stands and tavern folk;
in secretly neglecting their assigned posts
and hiding pretexts in selfish pursuits that evoke
a disregard of orders by others. For this Detachment,
a warrant of vagary: an offence to this command,
if each member does not report to their Sergeant
with due respect; if Shields will not faithfully stand
unified with the Company, encouraging turmoil
against the common good; in disobedience to stay
by Wiser, Robinson, Colter, and Boyle;
and R. Fields, separately, in refusing to obey.
Captain Lewis's Order was a measured opinion:
To value personal and public bonds in unison.[xxvii]

ENDNOTES

i. Julius S. Scott, *The Common Wind: Afro-American Currents in the Age of the Haitian Revolution* (Verson, 2018).

ii. Thomas Jefferson, *Notes on the State of Virginia* (University of North Carolina Press, Stockton edition, 1787/1982), 43-44.

iii. Specifics on the Lenape customs, clothing, and bead work are attributable to various online sources, and particularly to those from First Nations' on their traditional tribe's cultural heritage: e.g., www.delawaretribe.org.

iv. Gary E. Moulton, ed., *The Journals of the Lewis & Clark Expedition*, Volume 2, (University of Nebraska Press, 1986), 133-34.

v. Moulton, *Journals*, Vol. 2, 134-40.

vi. Moulton, *Journals*, Vol. 2, 140-41.

vii. Moulton, *Journals*, Vol. 2, 140-41.

viii. Moulton, *Journals*, Vol. 2, 141.

ix. Moulton, *Journals*, Vol. 2, 141.

x. Moulton, *Journals*, Vol. 2, 141-42.

xi. Moulton, *Journals*, Vol. 2, 142.

xii. Moulton, *Journals*, Vol. 2, 142.

xiii. Moulton, *Journals*, Vol. 2, 144-45.

xiv. Moulton, *Journals*, Vol. 2, 145-52.

xv. Moulton, *Journals*, Vol. 2, 150-53.

xvi. Moulton, *Journals*, Vol. 2, 153-54.

xvii. Moulton, *Journals*, Vol. 2, 154-56.

xviii. Moulton, *Journals*, Vol. 2, 156-57.

xix. Moulton, *Journals*, Vol. 2, 159-64.

xx. Moulton, *Journals*, Vol. 2, 164-66.

xxi. Moulton, *Journals*, Vol. 2, 166-67.

xxii. Moulton, *Journals*, Vol. 2, 166-68.

xxiii. Moulton, *Journals*, Vol. 2, 172-74.

xxiv. Moulton, *Journals*, Vol. 2, 161.

xxv. Mark B. Hamilton, "The Work Songs of the Voyageurs," H*istory Magazine*, Summer Issue (2021): 54-59.

xxvi. Friedrich Wilhelm Baron von Steuben, *Regulations for the Order and Discipline of the Troops of the United States, 1779; Baron von Steuben's Revolutionary War Drill Manual: A Facsimile Reprint of the 1794 Edition* (Dover Publications, 1985).

xxvii. Moulton, *Journals*, Vol. 2, 178-79.

BIBLIOGRAPHY

Hamilton, Mark B. "The Work Songs of the Voyageurs." *History Magazine*, Summer Issue (2021): 54-59. Note: Supporting research, "Vertical files for Mary Agnes Starr recording of French voyageur songs as sung by Reuben Valley." Folk Life Archives, Library of Congress, (July 2021). AFC1952/016.

Jefferson, Thomas. *Notes on the State of Virginia*. University of North Carolina Press, Stockton edition, 1787/1982.

Moulton, Gary E., ed. "Wintering at Camp Dubois: December 13, 1803 – May 14, 1804." In *The Journals of the Lewis & Clark Expedition*, Vol. 2, University of Nebraska Press, 1986.

Scott, Julius S. *The Common Wind: Afro-American Currents in the Age of the Haitian Revolution*. Verson, 2018.

von Steuben, Friedrich Wilhelm Baron. *Regulations for the Order and Discipline of the Troops of the United States*, 1779; *Baron von Steuben's Revolutionary War Drill Manual: A Facsimile Reprint of the 1794 Edition*. Dover Publications, 1985.

ADDITIONAL SELECTIONS

Background Sources:

Jackson, Donald, ed. *Letters of the Lewis and Clark Expedition with Related Documents*, 1783-1854. University of Illinois Press, 1962.

Vest, Jay Hansford C. "Will-of-the-Land: A Philosophy of Wilderness Praxis and Environmental Ethics." PhD diss., University of Montana, 1984. VDM Verlag Dr. Mueller, 4 January 2011.

Warren, Robert Penn. *Brothers to Dragons*. LSU Press, Revised edition (1951) October 1, 1996.

Articles by the Author:

"Introduction: 'An Oral History of the Mammoth in North America.'" *We Proceeded On*, Vol. 42, No. 3 (August 2016): 28.

"Northern Watersnakes: *Nerodia sipedon sipedon*, on the Lower Missouri River…." *Bulletin of the Chicago Herpetological Society*, Vol. 38, No. 11 (November 2003): 220-221.

"A Purely Literary Expedition: The Death of Sergeant Charles Floyd of the Lewis and Clark Expedition as Perceived by Captains Lewis and Clark." T*he Heritage of the Great Plains: Bicentennial Edition*, (May 2004): 41-62.

Media by the Author:

"The Art of Eco-Poetry: Strengthening the Dynamic in Response to Environmental Crisis," ASLE Annual (Virtual) Conference: EMERGENCE/Y, Emergent Environments Stream/River, Eugene, OR, 19 min., 08 sec., July 26-August 6, 2021, by Association of Literature and Environment, http://bit.ly/ASLE2021. Reposted September 2012 on "Mark B. Hamilton@earthsongs2013 Videos."

Discovering Home: A Sojourn On The Lewis And Clark Trail By Paddle And Pack Mule, video, Robert McConnell Productions, Gig Harbor, OR, January 2001, 37 min., 51 sec.

"www.youtube.com/@earthsongs2013." 59 video clips along the Lewis and Clark Return Route: Fort Clatsop to St. Louis, March to September 2001, posted 2013.

ABOUT THE AUTHOR

Mark B. Hamilton earned the BA and MA in English & Comparative Literature at San Diego State University, and the MFA in Creative Writing/Poetry at the University of Montana. He has published four poetry volumes and three chapbooks. His poems often focus on the riparian zone of American rivers, where he has traveled extensively by kayak and rowing dory as an outdoor enthusiast and environmentalist. His scholarly interests in the Lewis and Clark Expedition span three decades, and remain the backdrop for developing an eco-poetics in response to climate change.

His researched essays have appeared in: *The Heritage of the Great Plains, The Bulletin of the Chicago Herpetological Society, We Proceeded On,* and *History Magazine,* with inclusion into the Folk Life Archives, US Library of Congress. He has also edited two academic environmental journals: *Words On Wilderness*, University of Montana, and *Groundwork: a natural incentive,* Ball State University.

Mr. Hamilton taught writing, literature, and editing at Ball State University and Missouri Western State University for twenty years, and was a Visiting Research Faculty Member, Department of History, at Portland State University. Honors include a Matthew Hansen Endowment for Wilderness Studies, Literary Fellowships at UCROSS Foundation and The Sitka Center for Art & Ecology, two NEA Administrative State Grants for Visiting Artists to the South Madison Street Community Center, Muncie, IN, teaching and mentoring awards, campus and community developmental grants, and state, national, and independent recognitions for poetry. Additionally, he has been a journeyman shipwright and a caseworker for Children & Youth Services.

His creative works are the means to an inner activism in response to the climate crisis, and represent a turning away from the purely anthropocentric point of view, toward a more communal, inclusive, and cooperative value system for living on this Earth, this planet, in the natural world of our only and forever home.

For additional author information, view his website: MarkBHamilton.WordPress.com.

Or connect directly with him via email: markhamilton98643@yahoo.com.

www.ingramcontent.com/pod-product-compliance
Lightning Source LLC
LaVergne TN
LVHW090535110826
845146LV00003B/1110

* 9 7 9 8 8 9 9 9 0 4 2 2 6 *